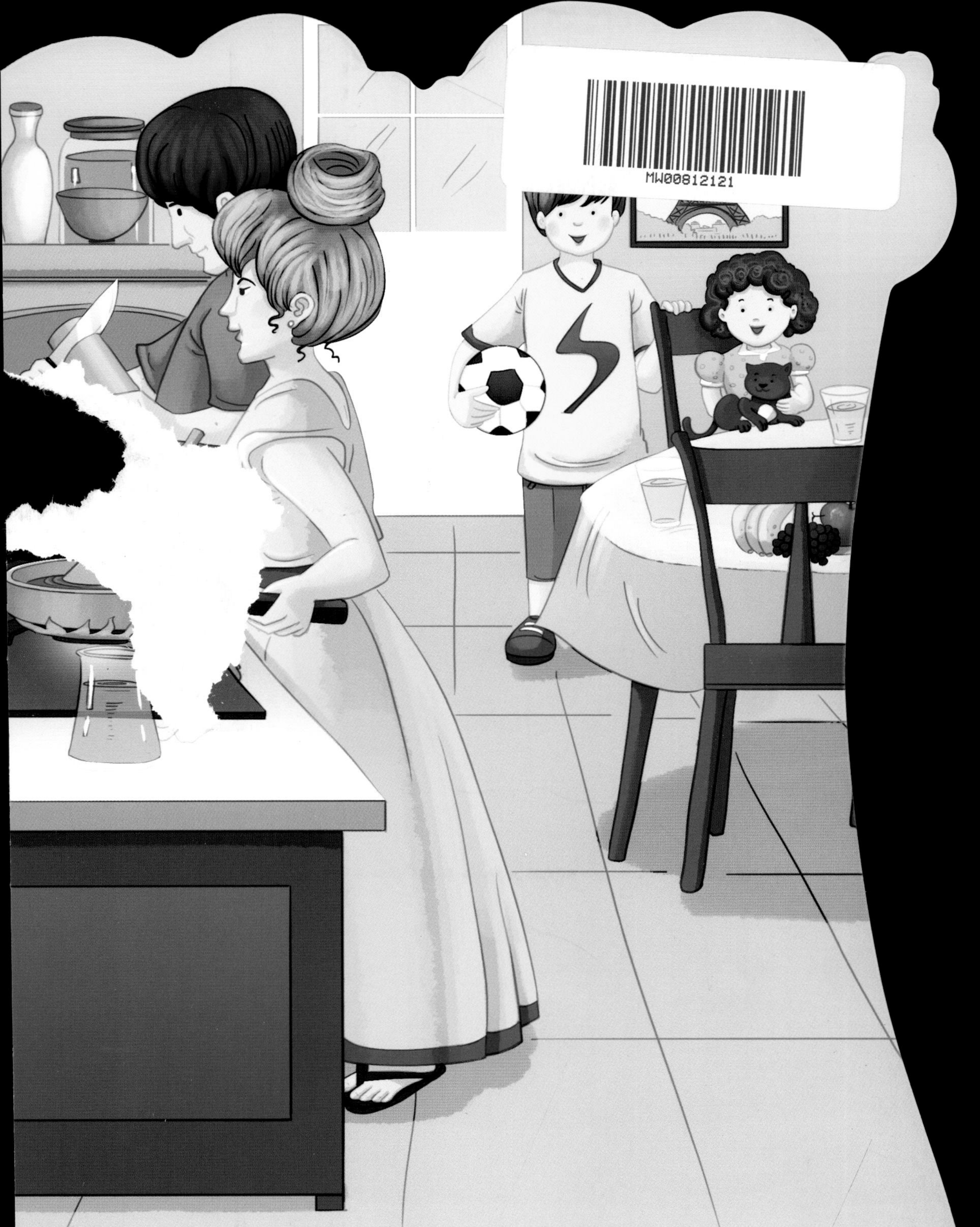

## THE EIFFEL TOWER

'Hurray! Our football team has won and I scored the most goals,' Austin said excitedly. 'And our ballet group also has won,' chirped his little sister, Chloe.

'Our kids deserve something special. How about taking them to the Eiffel Tower this weekend?' Their father smiled proudly at their mother.

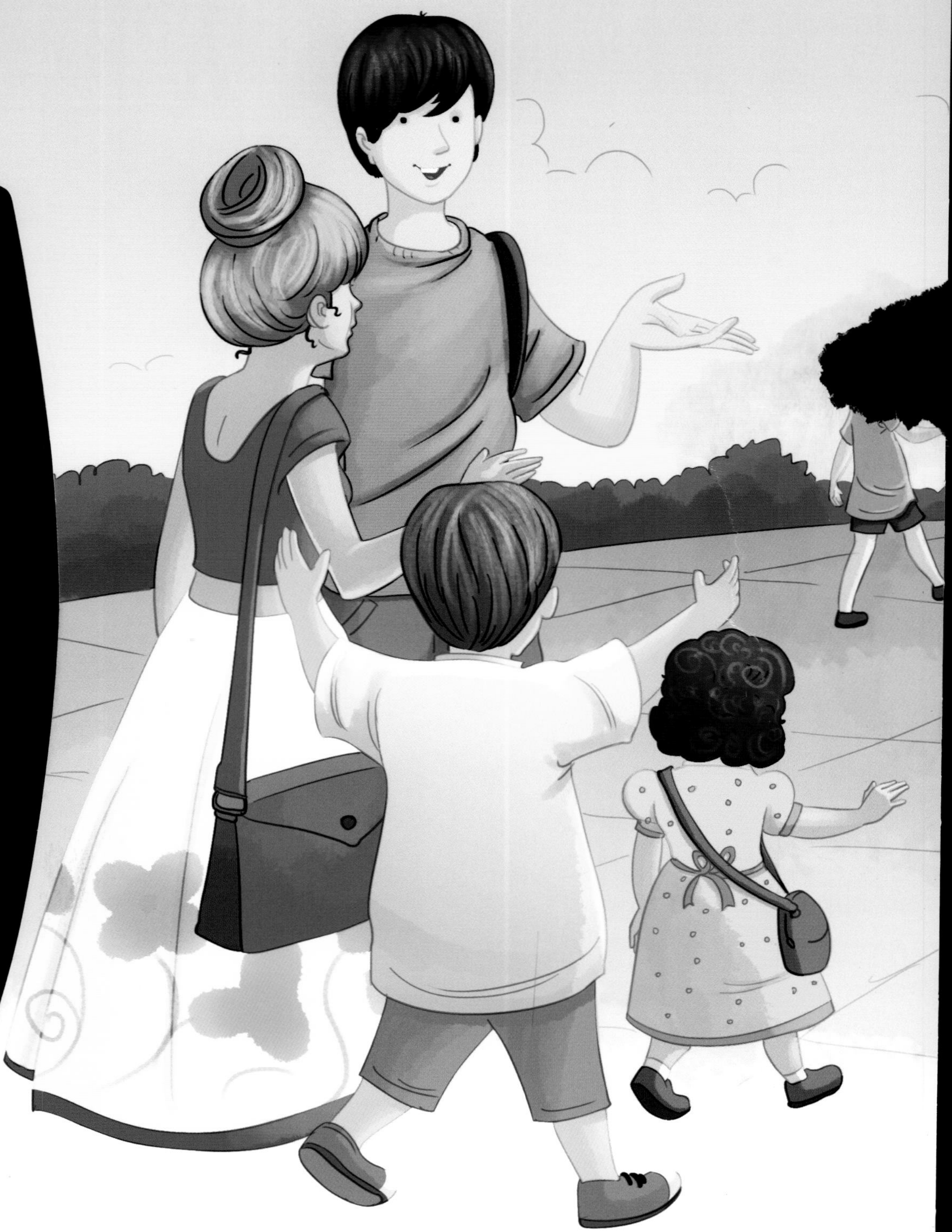

'My friends from other countries say I'm lucky to be living in Paris right where the Eiffel Tower is! They can only dream of visiting it.' Chloe smiled.

'Yes,dear. It's indeed our most famous landmark and the most-visited paid monument in the world,' Louise replied.

'It was designed and built by Gustave Eiffel's company. At first it was considered the ugliest building in Paris, but now it is the city's symbol,' Victor said as the four walked towards the famous tower.

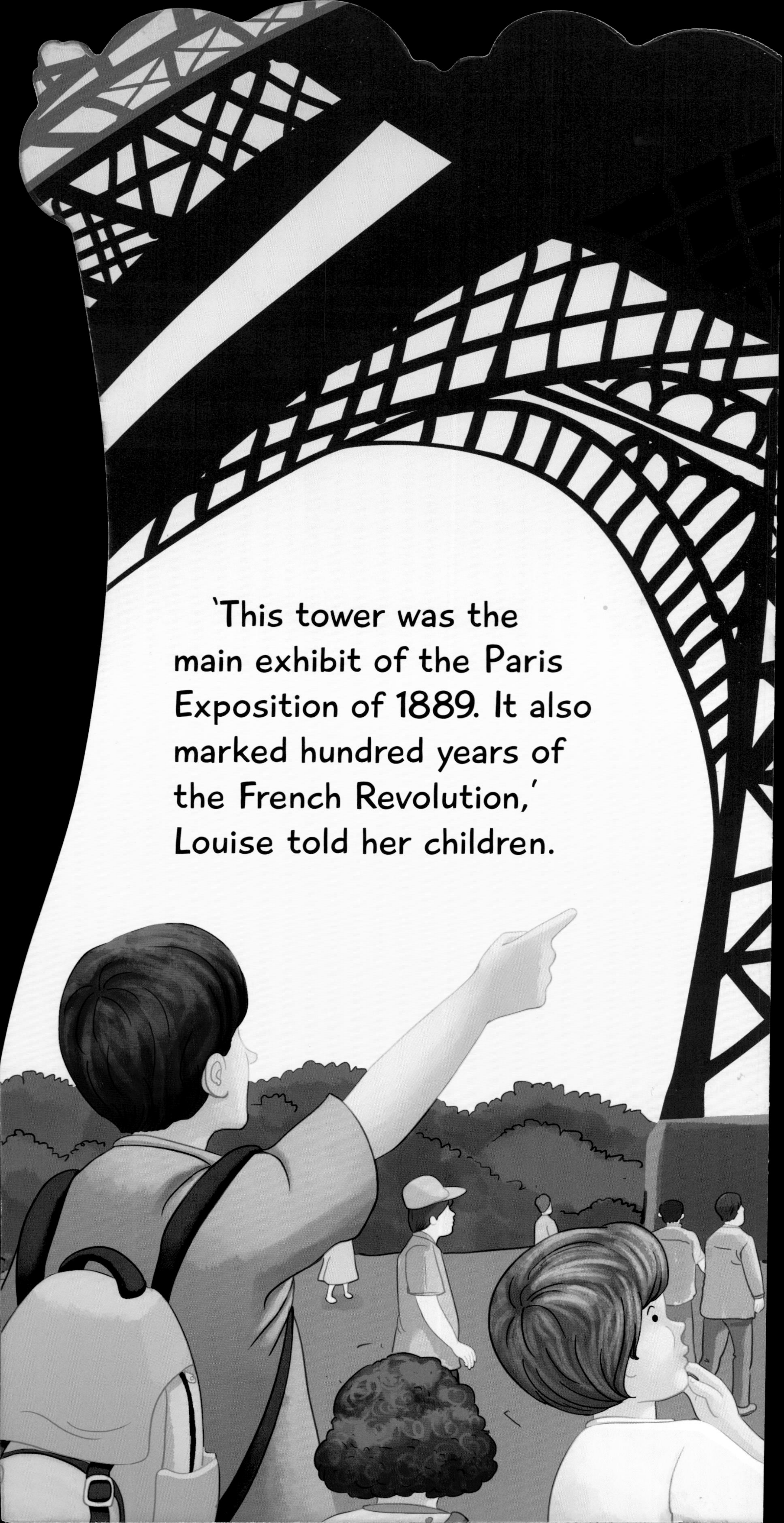
'This tower was the main exhibit of the Paris Exposition of 1889. It also marked hundred years of the French Revolution,' Louise told her children.

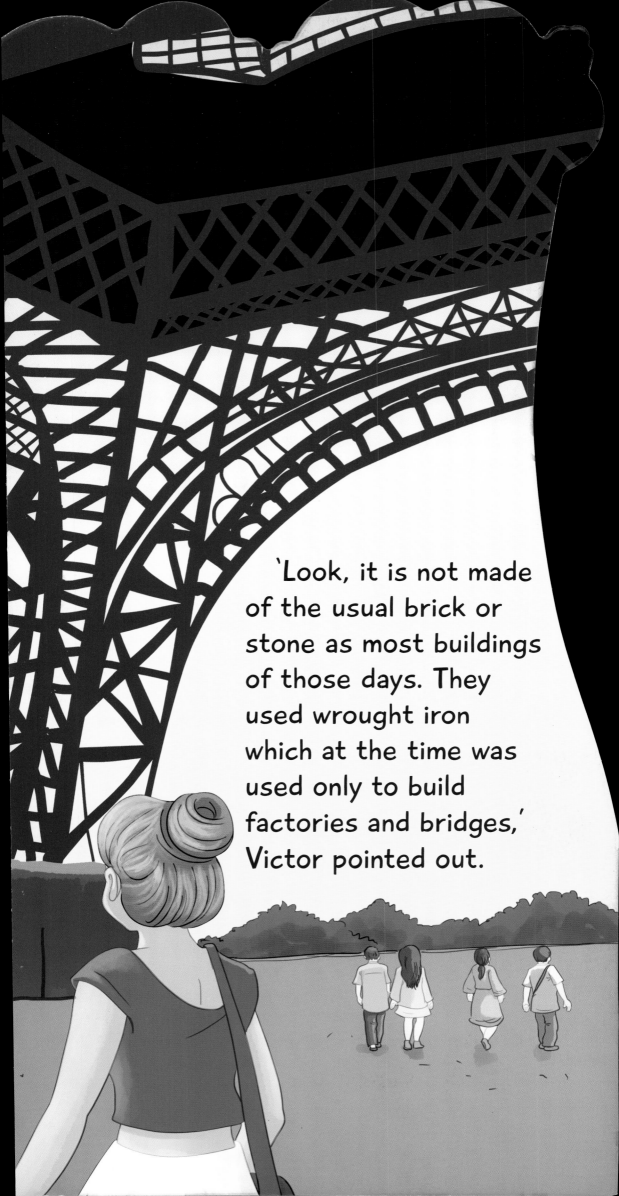

'Look, it is not made of the usual brick or stone as most buildings of those days. They used wrought iron which at the time was used only to build factories and bridges,' Victor pointed out.

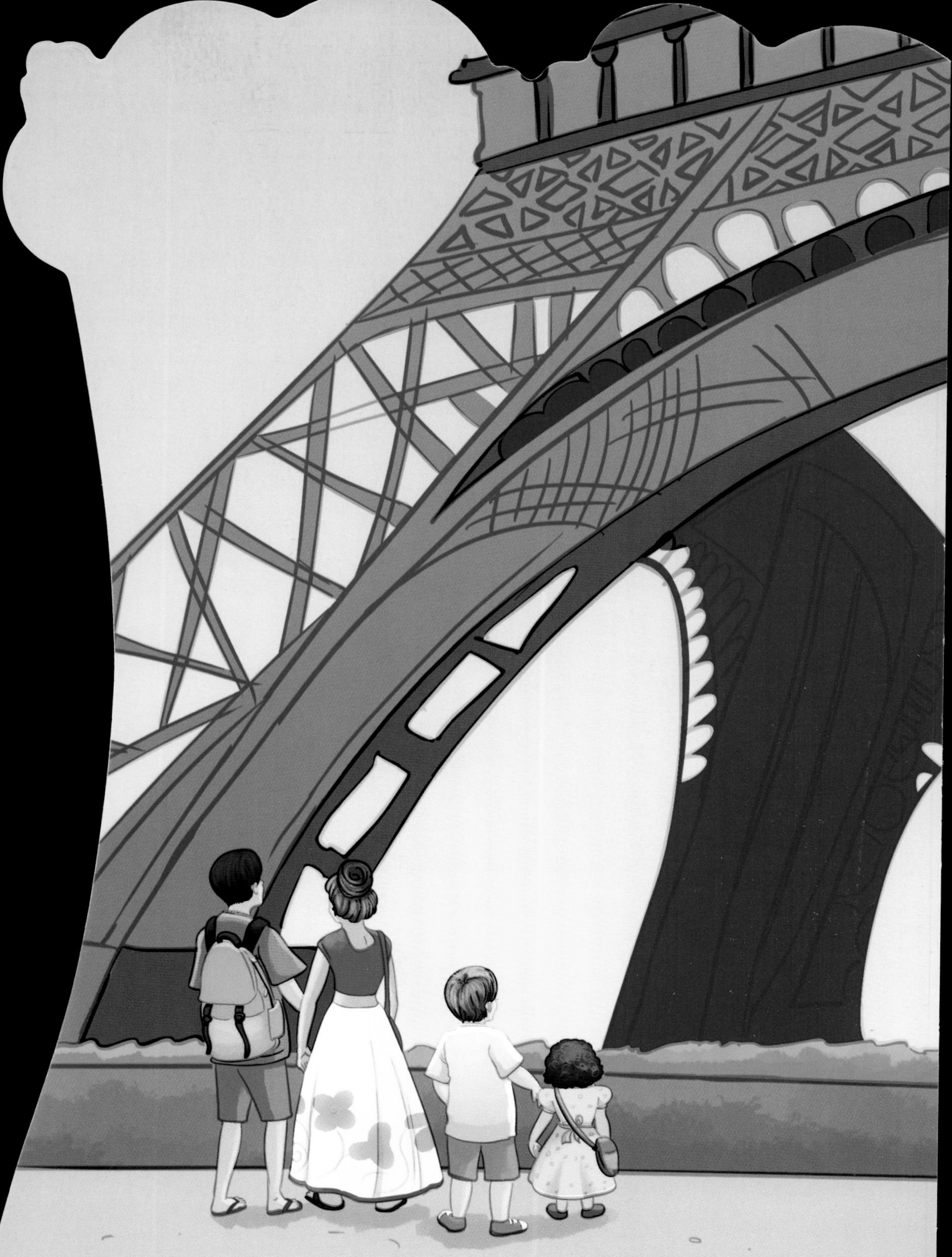

'But why doesn't the iron rust, dad?' Austin wanted to know.

'Good question, Austin. That's why every inch has been covered with tons of paint to avoid rusting. It's been repainted eighteen times already,' Victor answered.

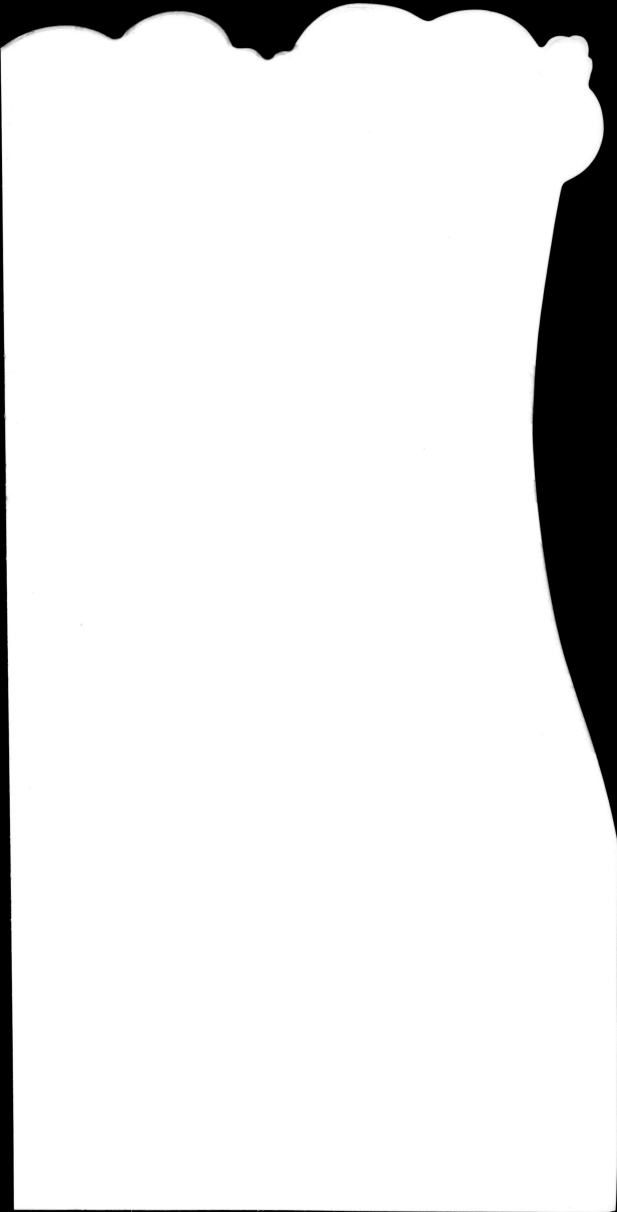

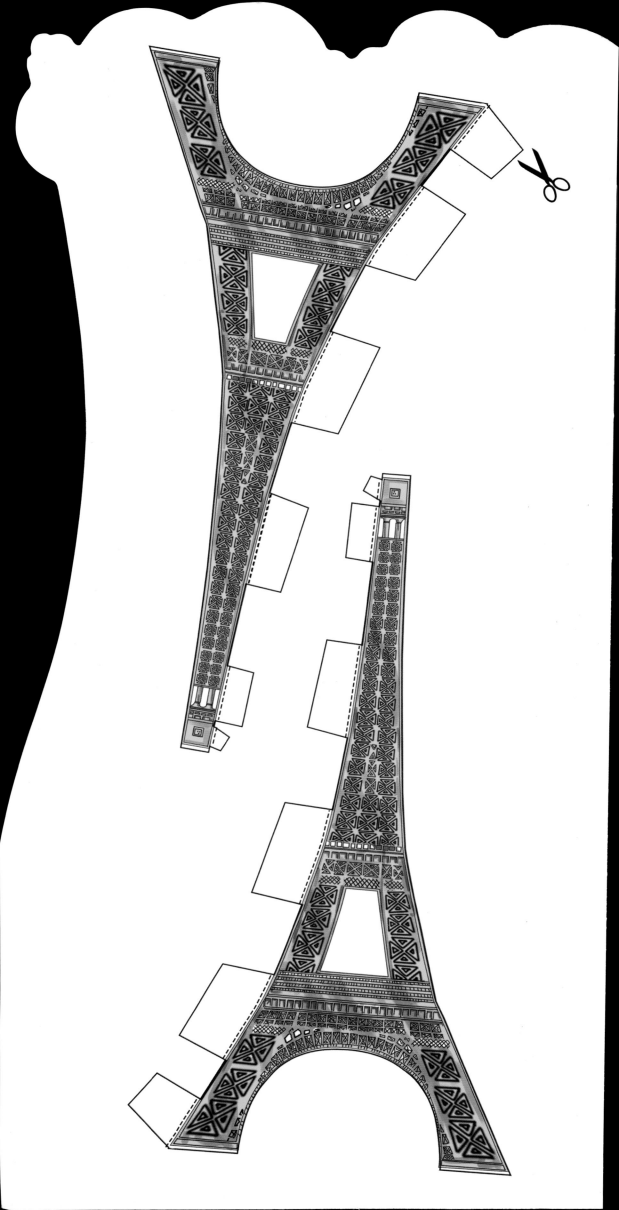

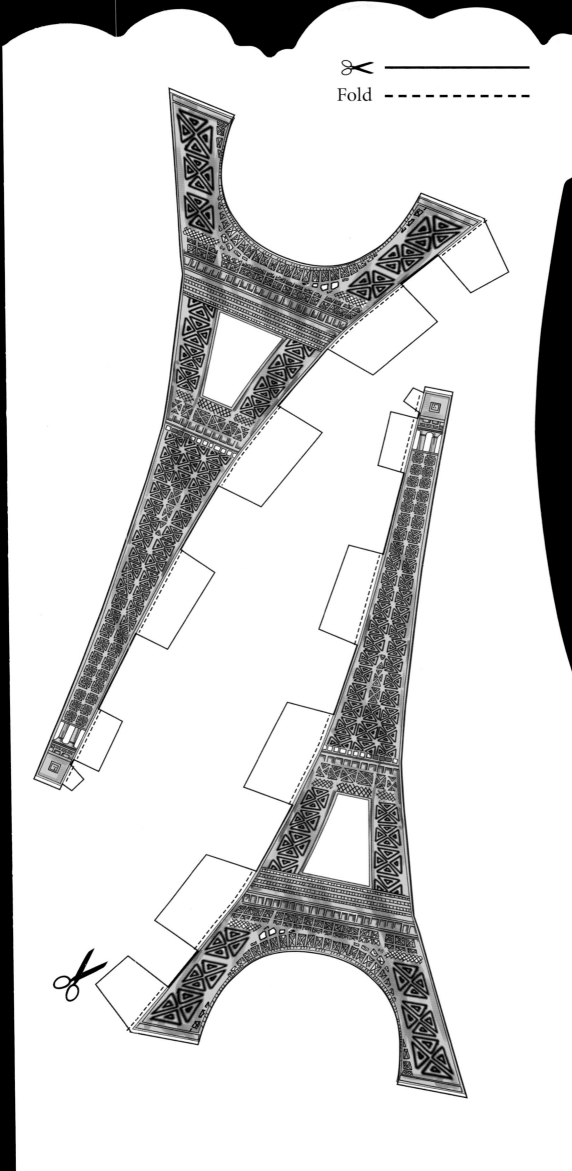

✄ ━━━━━━━━━━
Fold ╌╌╌╌╌╌╌╌╌

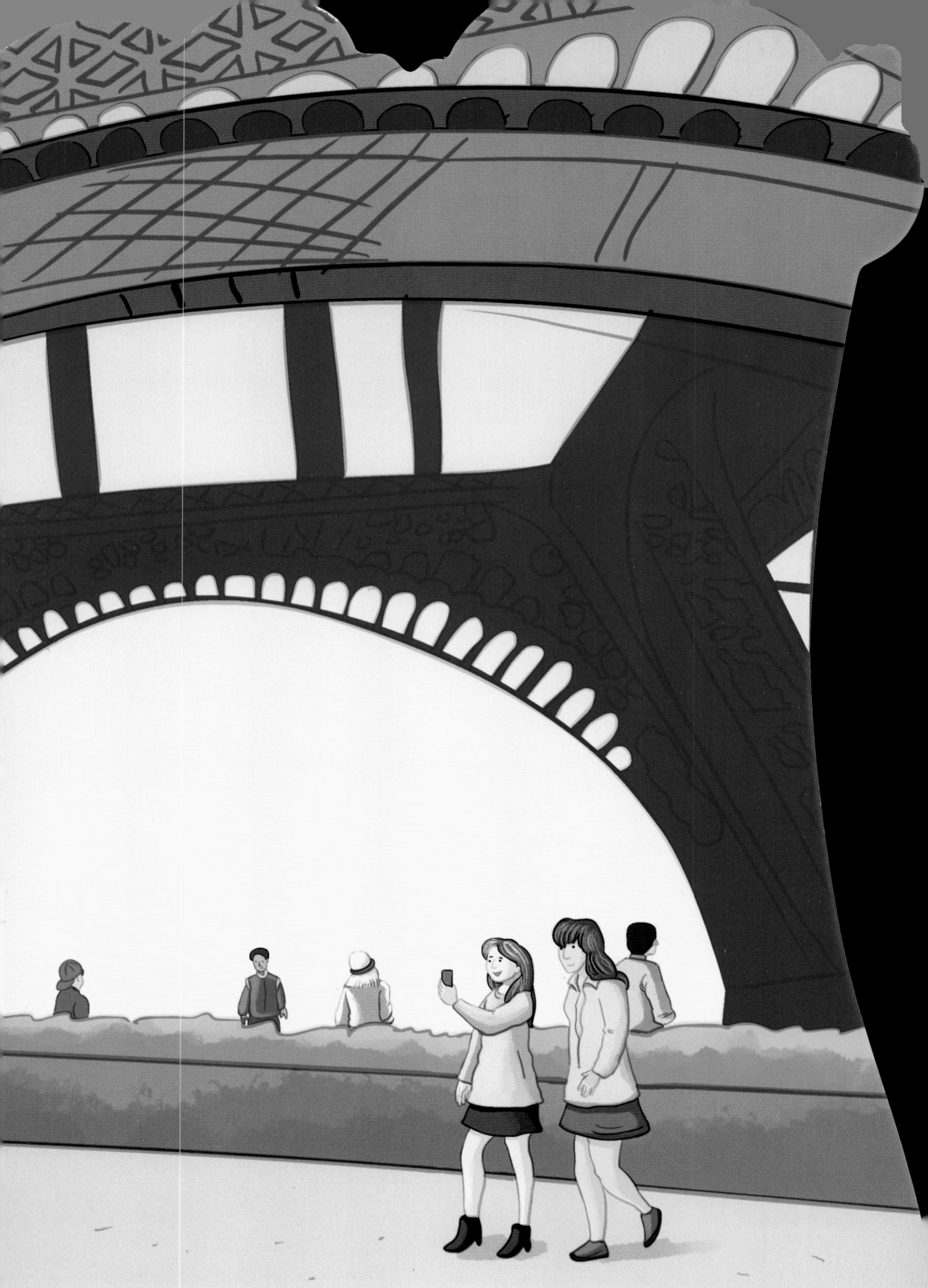

'You know, they were to bring down the tower in 1909, but then used it as a giant radio antenna, and now even digital television signals are transmitted from here,' Victor added.

'The tower is so high. How will we ever climb to the top?' wondered Chloe.

'Don't worry. There are lifts to reach the top,' Victor assured his daughter.' In fact, two of the original lifts are still working,' he added.

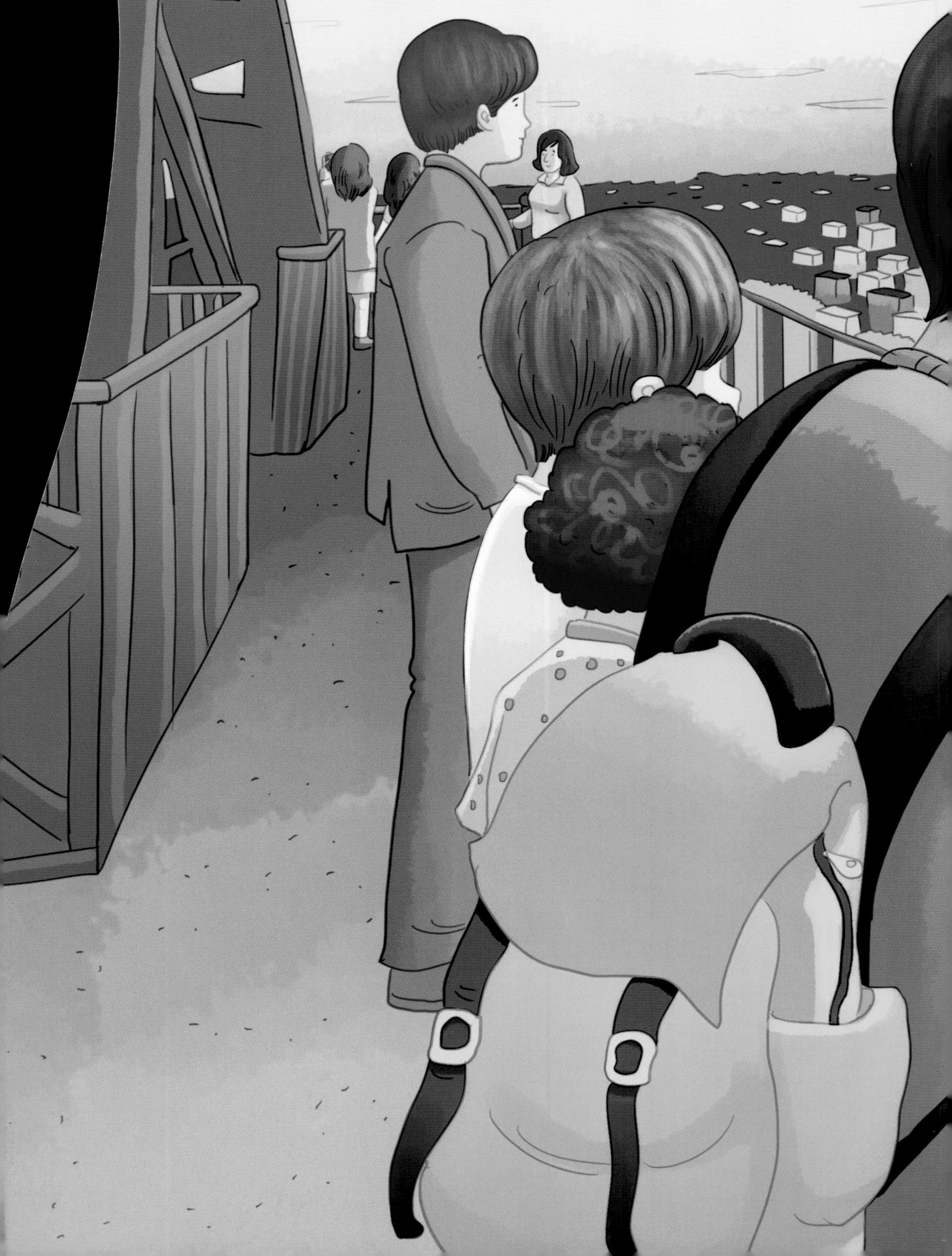

'Eiffel used a small apartment on the third floor to entertain friends and to perform experiments,' Louise quipped after they stepped out of the lift.

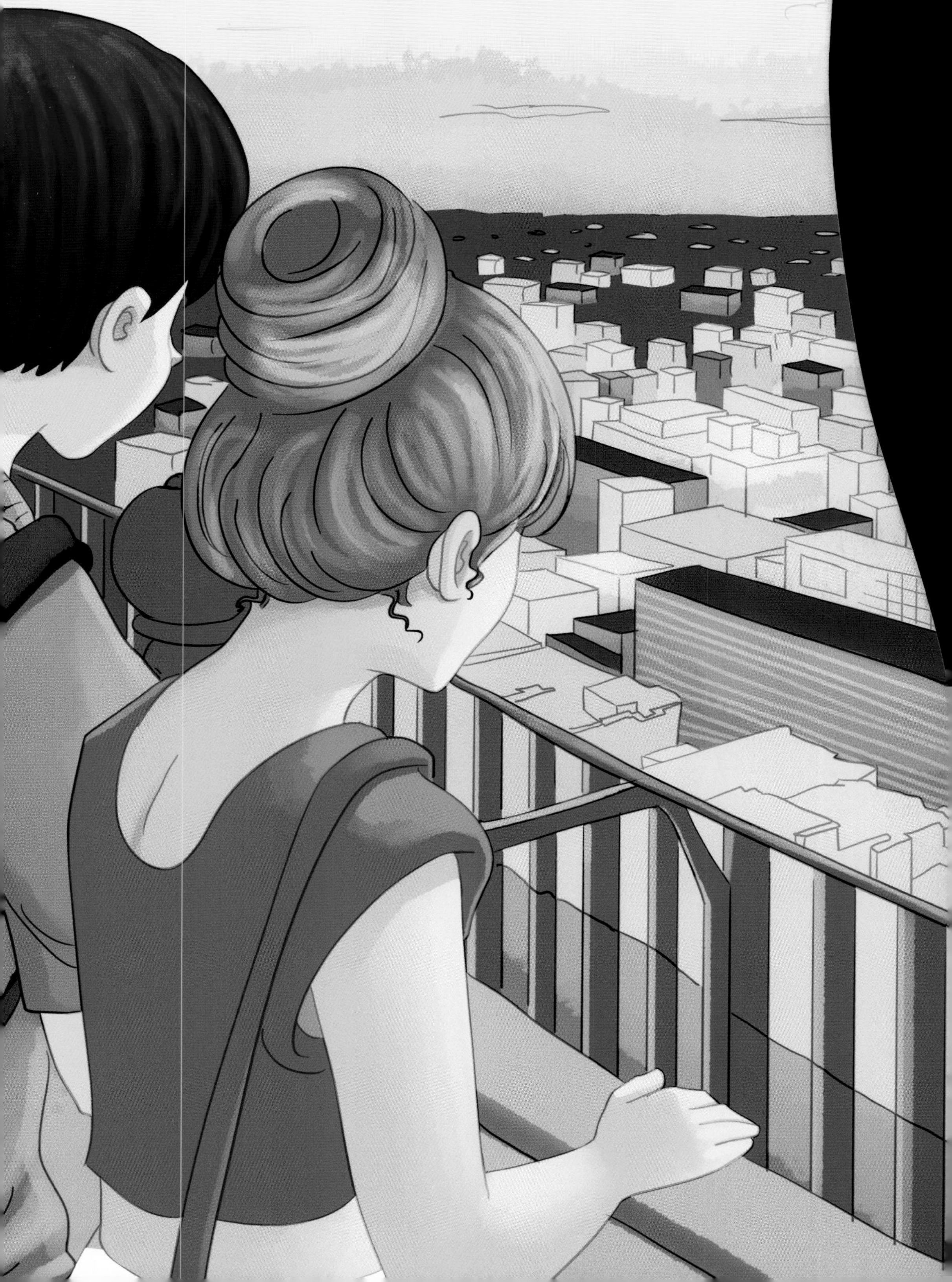

'Can you see the names of the 72 people who helped in building the tower engraved there?' Louise pointed towards the first balcony.

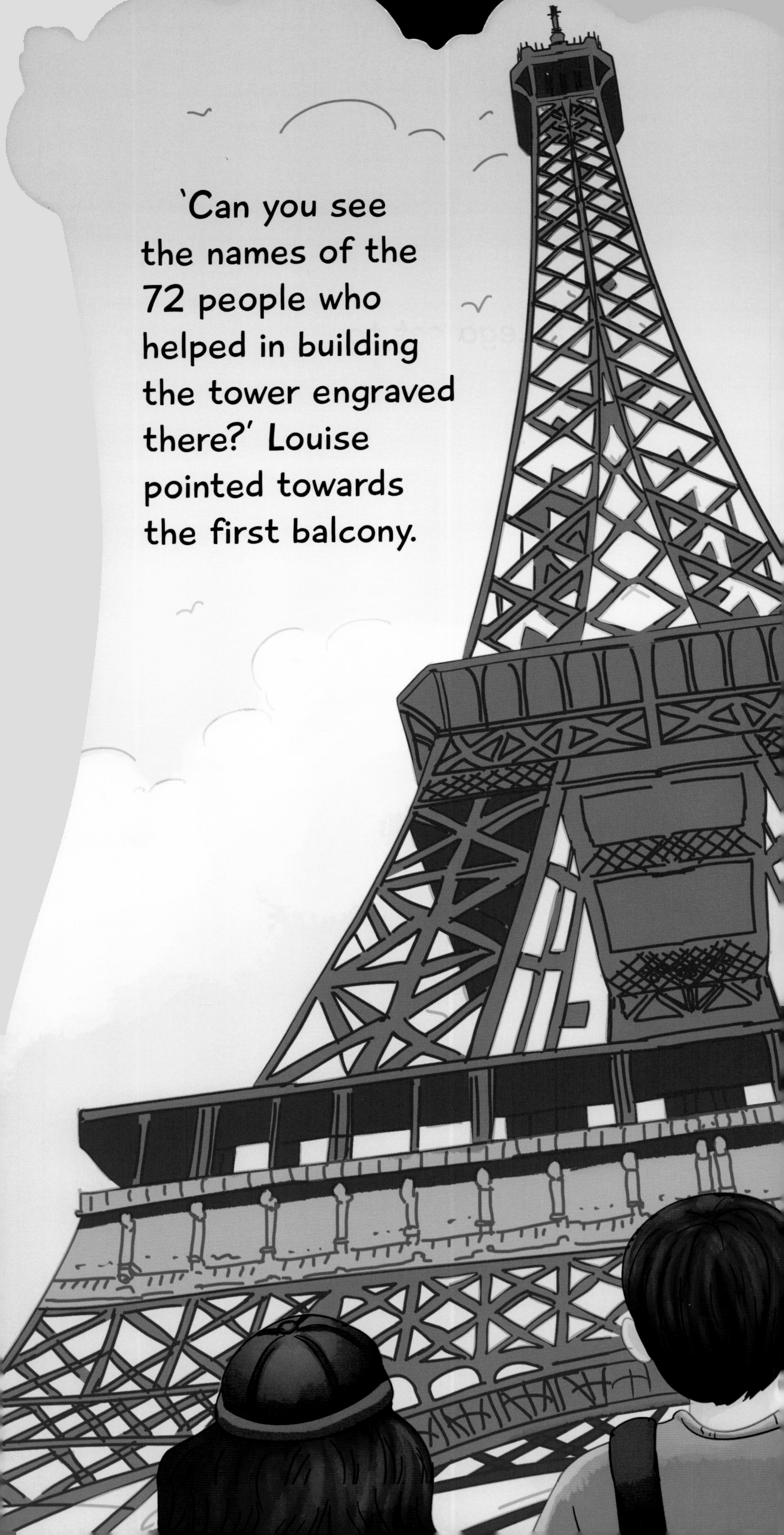

'I've decided to buy a Lego set to build my own Eiffel Tower and keep it in my room,' Austin said aloud.

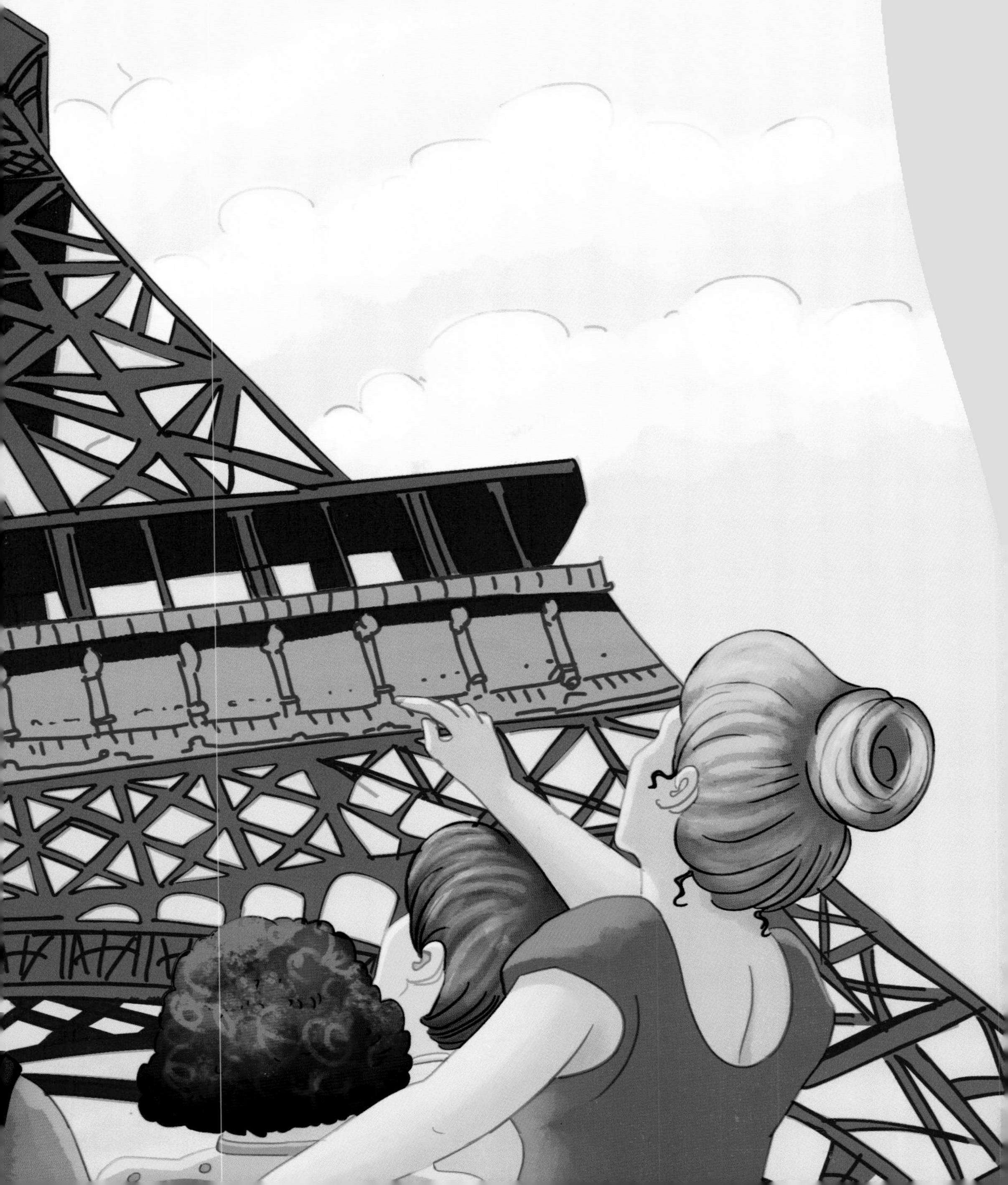

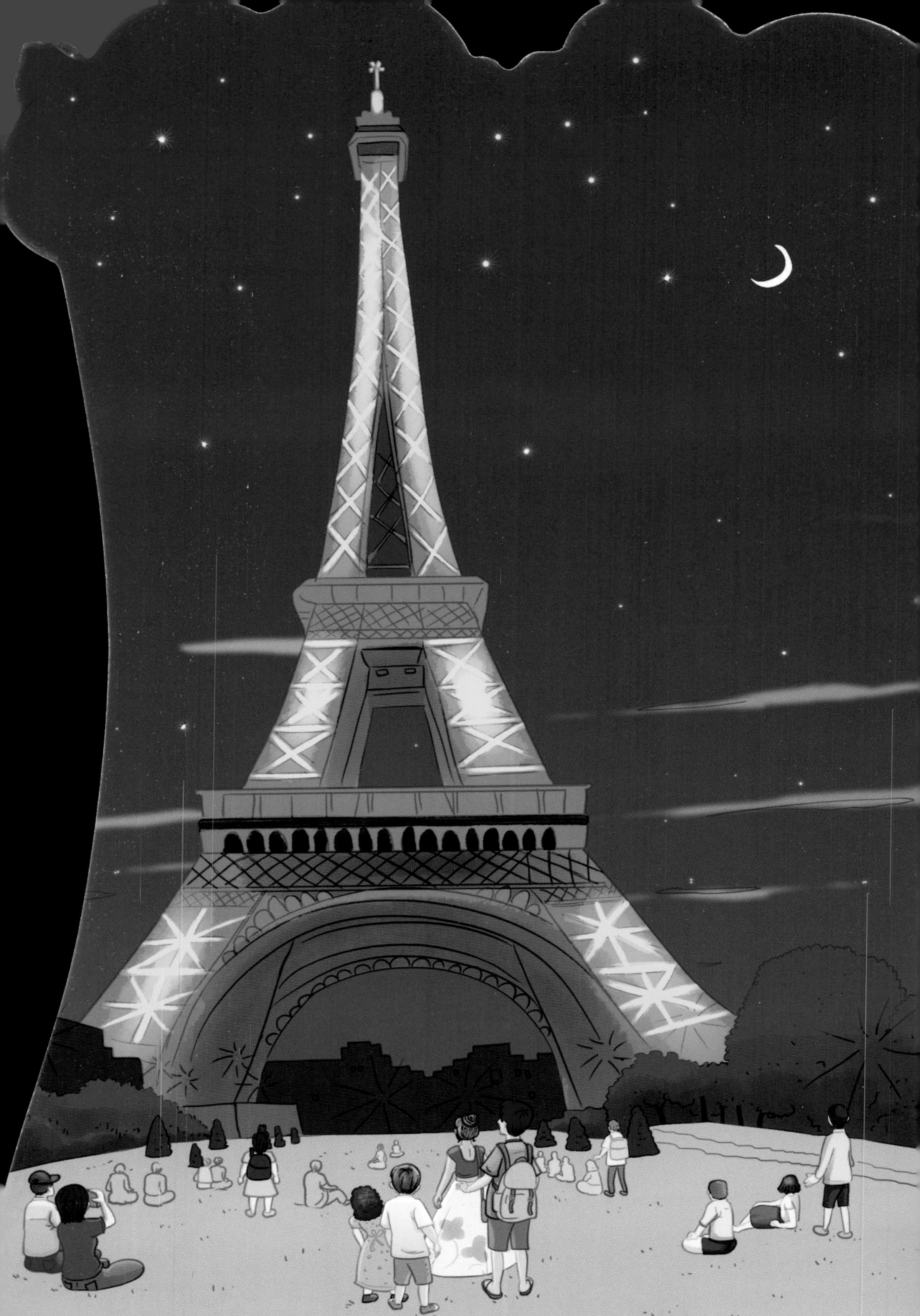

'Look, look, it's time for the Illumination Show,' Austin jumped excitedly.

'The tower is sparkling like a Christmas tree!' Chloe said with wide-eyed wonder.

'What an experience! We must come here again and again,' both children said to their parents.